BECAUSE *of* THE SANDS *of* TIME

ALSO BY ORO LYNN BENSON

Love, Death, and Flowing Water

BECAUSE *of* THE SANDS *of* TIME

Oro Lynn Benson

ABIQUIU PRESS

ISBN 978-1-7328237-4-7
Published by Abiquiu Press
abiquiupress@gmail.com

Text is set in Adobe Garamond Pro
Designed by Ginger Legato
Printed in the United States of America

I dedicate this book to my family and my friends. You carried me when I could not walk. You held my hand when I felt lonely. You laughed at me when I took myself too seriously. You laughed with me when the joy poured over us and washed us clean.

CONTENTS

PART I

PART TWO

PART FIVE

THE BEGINNING OF THE KALI YUGA

As her hundred sons lay dead on the battlefield, Gandhari confronted Krishna, saying, "You could have prevented this! Was I not faithful to you?" She cursed him that his town and all its inhabitants would be destroyed. He and all his descendants would die as her sons had died. Krishna calmly acknowledged that the curse would come to pass, not merely because she had been faithful but because of the sands of time.

She is not merely powerful

She is power

At peace

The grounding of rock bottom

The knowledge that nothing will last

In the river of endless change

In a life that flows from death

She builds with the pieces of shattered dreams

She builds from absolute strength

Because she is never not broken

As summers grow warmer
The lake heats
The algae blooms

We will not swim

The river still sings
Though the water is brown

Beavers and cormorants
Ride the currents

Summer is still
Achingly beautiful
Snakes slither among wildflowers
Squirrels gnaw my sheets
To make nests

Life in its abundance

Yet the whisper grows stronger
Almost audible
"Something is wrong"

Our lives are built of small moments
A single cloud rests in the pale dawn sky
A rooster punctuates morning bird calls
The cool air tiptoes into my bedroom
From the open door
My old cat sleeps beside me
In a puddle of the urine
He can no longer control

My mind chews on this problem
All the solutions unacceptable
The light shifts as the sun climbs into the day
My eyelids droop
I would return to sleep
But for the smell of cat piss

Amid drama and trauma
Our lives build upon small moments

Dusk has softened the sun's hard brightness
I glimpse a mound of billowing whiteness
At the base of the pear tree
My first thought—"Angel"
Though my angels do not
Wear white feathers

A mound of turkey feathers
The coyote has taken my last turkey
A kick to my chest
A crime scene
An angel

I cannot bear to touch the feathers
Yet if I leave them they will haunt me
A hard rain wakes me in the night
The bands around my chest loosen
The feathers will be gone

Lie shattered around me
See how the shards
Glisten like jewels
In sunlight

Floating on my back
Resting on hot water
Sunlight caresses my face
The spring cradles my body

Wetness and warmth
Wrap me in pleasure
With the slightest thrill of danger
This gentle cushion could swamp me
Should I slip into the sleep that beckons

Joy and danger
Precisely balanced
The nature of Nature

Vast waves of pain
Breaking over me
I breathe
Then sink
Shocked by the betrayal

Gentle as the rabbits that wait
Below the ditch
Friendly as a picnic at the lake
I threw open the gates of my home
And my heart
Seduced by a smile and a joke
The box was emptied
The money gone

Why did I believe that a thief
Would be marked with a scowl
Or a furtive glance?
So foolish to expect
That evil would bear its mark
Upon its face

There was no warning sign:

danger

I walked the Red Wash
For more than thirty years
The shortcuts I took became paths
That others followed
Year by year those shortcuts
Grew deep
The water races down
Where it used to flow in great curves

It tears at the land
Then leaves it dry and barren

I did not mean for my steps to do harm
Never imagined that my footprints
Would have an impact
Never thought of others
Who would follow

How is it possible?

The past, past

This

Now

Fresh

Bright

Forgiveness given

And received

Again and again

We do what we can
We are searching
In the dark

Years ago she told me
The trees were ceasing to talk to each other

Now the piñons stand mute on the hillside
Their needles dry and brown

The experts speak of
An infestation of bark beetles
It might be loneliness

The homeless
Standing on corners
Their signs
Their woe-filled eyes
Our children
Our friends
Their talent and sweetness
Shredded by addiction
In seeking comfort
They loosed demons

The old are ashamed
Hide the bruises
They nod out alone
In their homes
Their drugs prescribed
By doctors

Should they be swept
Under and away

For the young
Who have enough energy
To embrace the wild ride
The mind can entirely fragment

They may pass through madness
On their slide toward death

Some I love are on this journey
I pray they do not die tonight

CHANGE

Who will not die
Cannot change

Who cannot change
Is already dead

I know some who begin with open hearts
Live in delight
Tied to this world by love

They also know anguish
Feel the dying of the waters
The growing silence of the trees
The fire in those addicted to power and plenty
This is not a gentle age
It can crush an open heart

Some withdraw
They watch from the sidelines
Some are given labels
And told to take their medications

Some after long wandering
And much struggle
Wash up on the shore of Spirit

Move the locus of power

Through the aura

Under the barrier of the skin

Into the self

To the center of Being

The rhythm of the river
Pulsing like my heart

Light in the sky
And on the mesas

The cat in the doorway
Waiting for a lizard

Each singing a song of joy

On the riverbank
Watching the flames dance
In the fireplace

Fire and water
Perfect beauty
Infinite tension
They cannot merge
Only one would survive
I sit in the space between

The night waits in stillness
While the flames leap
To the river's lullaby

A blanket of darkness
Rolls out over the land

The river disappears
Its voice grows louder

So it has been
Nights beyond numbering

The night is crisp black
Sharp black
Winter-sky black
I grope
For the latch

Winter stars
Burn in the ebony canopy
Points of light
Piercing
Penetrating
Exploding in the darkness
Alive in the night

Black calves silent
Along the fence line

Each day they walk
Through the winter grass

Morning sun
Sets the grass aglow

The sky fills with honking of geese
But the clamor is held aloft

It cannot disturb the silence
Of the night-black calves
Or the light-filled grass

Morning sun glistens on
White trunks of cottonwoods
Against an ice-blue sky

My granddaughter in her flamingo-pink swimsuit
Rests upon willow-green water
Floating from her mother's arms to mine

I drive from the mountains at sunset
The horizon glows fire
Above black hills

Each day offers gifts
Of beauty, joy, and love

Mingled with each day's measure
Of grief, loss, and pain

I work to hold the balance
When young, I worked with passion
At maturity, with desire and careful plans
In age, with acceptance

Joy and sorrow fuse together
We learn to embrace the joy
Without demanding an end to sorrow

A meal fit for the gods
When times get tough on Olympus

A treat reserved for Sunday dinner
When our family of seven gathered
To feast on a single can of tuna
In a warm sauce made from
Flour, margarine, and milk
Ladled over saltines

The crunch of the savory cracker
Beneath a warm slurry
And the faint hint of fish

The taste

The thrift

The love

The Lord of Creation
Everything manifest pours forth
From His Being

His nature
Procreation

Shiva cursed him
Cut off one head
Pictures show him
Old, secluded, worried
He is rarely worshipped

Are we not grateful
To find ourselves alive?

Do we judge
The desire to reproduce?

Do we not wish to honor
The Creator
Being ourselves His creation?

Hyacinths
Purple and lavender
Just outside my door
The wild honking of geese
Flying upriver
In their ragged V
The world turns again
In its enduring cycles
The terror
That fills the news
And my heart
Seem distant and transitory

Like flax flowers
Bright blue in the morning breeze
But faded and turned in on themselves
In the afternoon sun

Like the plastic grocery sack
Caught on a log
Dancing in the river shallows

Like a calico cat
Waiting patiently
At the entrance
To a gopher hole

A virus is
Neither good nor bad
Neither friend nor enemy

Part of the always changing pattern
Of the shifts that mark
The passage of time
In the mind of God

In the face of turmoil
We begin again to pray
For those we love
For those who suffer
For frontline workers
We will never know

For humankind

We offer prayers of longing
Prayers of gratitude
We pray for the way things were
And the way they will be
We pray consciously
Lighting candles
Bowing heads
Feeling the enormity
Of change

We barely notice the prayer
We find we have been repeating
"Keep us safe"
"Heal them"
"Thank you"

Some of us kneel again
Where we have always knelt
Others have never
Asked the Divine for anything
We could not tell you
To whom or what we turn
We simply release our longing
Into the great heart of all Being

Surprised to find in the moment of prayer
In the moment of helplessness
The resonance of love

A small toad
Hiding in the bathroom
The scattered entrails
Of a gopher
Caught by the cat
An unfamiliar bug
Feet whirling
As it lies on its back
In my hand
The grasshopper horde
Clinging to the screen door

Life surrounds me
As I read
Of the rising number of deaths

We look into your face
Not beautiful
Yet beguiling
We are drawn
To your fierce strength
We are drawn
To the softness
At your core

What comes from misfortune?

Everything

In the West fires rage
In the East floods tear the land
We wait in our homes
Angry with each other
Afraid

I knew the term
Could not imagine
The meaning
Now I am beginning
To learn

For some, suffering is a teacher
For others, joy is a teacher
I studied in suffering's school

I wonder
Did I make a mistake?
Did I have a choice?

DANGER

Just below
The nattering mind
We remain children
Monsters under our beds

Gray-green hills
Deep green trees
Dry brown grasses
The early winter palette
Driving sixty miles per hour
My focus is on the road

Suddenly
At the edge of my vision
A flash of red
My body tightens
Head pivots
Focus narrows

A deer carcass
Torn in half
Surrounded by
Five black vultures

My body feels
The warning

I know
Without thought
The color of trauma
Of danger
The color of death

It rests
In quiet dignity

I walk in the arroyo
Inhaling the calm
That flows down its flanks
Toward the river

CHOICE

Arching over every moment
Choice births destiny

First tearing, then sealing
The shape of time

Futures forged
In a moment

We are bound to
The deep well of Silence
Whence flows
All action

Endlessly erupting

We struggle
For attention
For survival
For impact
For success
For love

While the Silence abides

The days have piled
One on the other
For more than forty years
Small shifts
Have grown into
Colossal changes

Toddlers are now parents
Vibrant young hippies
Are now wizened and bent

Impossible dreams
Have become inevitabilities
While some visions
Have dissolved

And I, the observer of these changes,
am equally changed

I can no longer
Drive at night
The lights
Of oncoming cars
Are hurtling spears
Glinting shards
That tear
Ripple
Shatter
The darkness

On the flagstone path
My toe caught
the frayed hem
of my pants

I plunged
toward the earth

The fall took a single second
But in the infinite
heart of that second

My mind filled with fear
I imagined
Broken bones
Blood on the path

Today I nurse
skinned knees
and a new awareness
of my frailty
A new connection
to an uncertainty
that waits quietly
In some future
that no longer
seems distant

There I was sitting on the stoop
When that old man walked up
His hair as white as mine

Most folks don't know shit about being old
They don't know about sinking down into the gentle quiet of memories
Or swinging out on the long rope of time into known and unknown worlds
They don't know about shuffling lives and selves
For the pure delight of feeling the flow of change

All they see is a couple of geezers talking
As the sun sinks in the sky
While its rays grow brighter
In their hearts

SENIOR CITIZEN'S DOWN DOG

We gather for yoga class
On Tuesday mornings
We don't wear yoga pants
We are a bit stiff
But still mobile

Perhaps because
We gather for yoga class
On Tuesday mornings

Beneath the surface
I find
Infinite connection
Nothing accidental
Nothing isolated
The ant I just stepped on
The woman in front of me
In the checkout line
The men I slept with
In my drinking days
The trees that whisper
In the morning's soft breeze
All connected
All creating each other

Source singing to Itself

As we climb the mountain
The road curls and twists
Around a blind curve
We come upon
An elk carcass
The ribs gleam white
The haunches hide covered
Eagles and ravens
Peck at the corpse

At our approach
The eagles
Rise in magnificent silence
Launch themselves into the sky

They carry messages
To the gods
Avoid humans
Soar on high currents

Ravens sit on branches,
Fence posts, and street signs
They carry messages
From gods to men

Rise only slightly, then settle back
Enjoy the feast
Unchallenged
By their regal cousins

The hawk's screech
Cuts the morning silence
Insistent, fearsome

The turkey poults stand frozen
The tom turkey issues a retort
Never has his gobble sounded so futile

This is not a shouting match
But a battle against swooping talons
The turkeys will lose

GRIEF

The ones I love
Will keep dying
And I will keep
Missing them

I see
White smoke
In the pines
Only a small plume
But my stomach tightens
My breath freezes in my lungs

I have never seen a forest fire
Yet I know the terror
We all know the terror
In the West
We know
What we have never seen

Fire

We cut the brush near our homes
We know where our important papers sit
We consider what we would take with us
Should we flee

Today the air is thick
I cannot see the far peaks
To the southwest a controlled burn
From the northwest smoke flows in from California

I pray to all my gods
Keep us safe
From fire

Chaos stalks the land
Flights are canceled
Computers crash
Unfamiliar phone numbers
Leave unintelligible messages

We live in an age
Shaped by Mercury
The winged messenger
The essence of
Modern life

Connecting
Talking
Thinking
Moving
Ever Faster

When Mercury turns backward
In the ancient sky
Our modern world upends itself

In the midst of that upheaval
We pause
Reflect
Search our own pasts
For understanding

When intellect fails
We call to our deeper selves
Not because we desire
To do so
But because we must

The present pours endlessly into the past
All creation expands to hold the deluge
We stand clutching the cup of self
Catching drops from the infinite tide

He has lived in his body
For nearly a century
It is stiff
His heart bursts with anger
Self-pity turns to cruelty
Cruelty to humiliation

Years of triumph
When sight and hearing were keen
When skills were honed and used
And strength flowed through his limbs

All gone

The past is sharp and taunts his frail frame
Thin air does not fill his lungs
Frozen meals offer little nourishment
TV replaces life
Which is slipping through his fingers

A fate worse than dying young

The fierce grip that sustained him
Has frozen into habit
He cannot let go

Hands that clutch happiness
Cannot open to hold joy

The struggle for happiness
Exhausts

Acceptance of sorrow
Opens us

To the compassion
Of Spirit

GOLDEN

Day slips toward night
I watch the cattails
Amber in the slanting light
Growing more golden each day
As fall edges into winter

A single goldfinch
Rests on one fluffed spike

The shadow of a magpie
Flying upriver
Felt before seen
Gone before known

Yet the balance
Of the morning
Is changed

Such is the sway
Of this trickster

She nests just upriver
Beyond the bend
Hidden in the high grass

Mornings and evenings
Her great wings carry her
Into sight

Thin legs
Trailing behind

Those great wings
Like angel's wings
But floppy

The hawk riding the breeze
Seeking
The pack rat settling into its nest
After a night of scavenging
The mosquito searching out
The warmth that means
Nourishment and perpetuation of lineage
The red racer slipping
Silently, smoothly
Into the earth

Each so completely itself
That no question is possible

Tonight there will be laughter in the hall
An end to sacrifice
For sacrifice is its own punishment
As compassion is its own reward

Let us release the arrogance of humility
Reveal our beauty and power without fear

At last we see that self-doubt diminishes the whole
Understand that empathy is self-knowledge set free

Let us hug and lean upon each other's shoulders
Let us laugh
Together

Let us dance

The trees have dropped their leaves
Gaunt skeletons against a dusky sky

Bird songs fill the air
A cascade of
Excitement, exuberance, and clarity

My eyes see a world slipping
Toward winter's rest

My ears delight
In the symphony
That celebrates
The transformation

They read the signs
Feel their meanings
Attend to the smallest indications

Then obey the commands
Bet everything
On the direction
Of the moment

We all gamble
With every breath

TODAY

Always now
Only now
Opening like a gift

I stand in the midst of symphony
The siren song of the river
Water rushing in its endless cycle
Mountain, sea, air
Repeat

The gentle rustle
Of the cottonwoods
As they watch me and my kind
Fret and race without considering
How quickly our time will pass

Lilt of the swallows
Raising their fledglings
In the mud nest on the wall
The squeak of my cat
Who yearns to reach them

Bullfrogs on the bank
Rooster greeting the sun
Hum of the refrigerator
Life in all its forms
And lessons

I stand in the center
Of the manifest world
I can never be alone
Amid all this energy
Calling to itself

The meaning lies in
The alchemy of the personal
All else is theory
Like fog above the meadow

What will we take
Beyond the tomb?
Only moments of
Experience
Essence of self

First pale glimmer of morning sun
Smell of last night's lamb stew
Lavender and garlic

I drink the smoke
Of burning pine branches
Rising through tea leaves

Logs smolder and glow
The vapor softens all bitterness

The magic of Lapsang Souchong

In China
I sit under cottonwoods
Sipping pine smoke
Filtered through a straw basket

A single light along the river
One firefly
Then another
And another

I know there are fields
Where hundreds dance
But these three are all I need
For ecstasy

My joy would fill the river
Crest the dams
All the way
To Big Bend

Very
Large
Geese
Float
Gently
Down
A
Very
Shallow
River

How
Do
They
Do
That?

MOMENT

My sense of time
Begins and ends with the moment
Always and only the moment

As a child, my moment was embedded
In a limitless flow of moments
Summer lasted forever
Winter even longer

As an elder, my moment is embedded
In a racing torrent

The twenty-first century
Has been shorter
Than the summers
Of my childhood

But the moment has always
Been of the same duration
Impossible to measure
Clearly infinite
Always and only now

I rest in silence
Inner voice muted

No thought arises
To speak over the hush

The sky dark
The earth darker still
The moon has set
The sun has not yet risen
I walk in the soft darkness
Within the promise of light

The crimson sunset
The double rainbow
The lightning flash
The superheroes
The dark villains

The excitement
Is only embroidery
On the surface
Of the tapestry
We weave
Of mundane thread

The tea steeping
Because I am out of coffee
The warm shower
When I could not wait
For hot
The joy of seeing my son
When he brings his son
To spend the afternoon
Music on the cell phone
In my pocket
As I walk to the ditch

The endless parade
Of average moments

Life built slowly
Consistently
Persistently
The small

The normal
Ours

Where it all
Really happens

Waiting in line
At the pearly gates
Shuffling with irritation
And anxiety
While Jehovah and Lucifer
Sit in judgment

We suddenly realize
We have misunderstood
Everything

God is not the white-robed
White-haired
White-skinned
Elder
Who offered comfort and success
If we would follow the rules

That is Lucifer

Jehovah is the handsome
Reddish fellow
With the horns

The one who led us
Ever deeper
Ever farther
Into questions
About our natures
And our paths
He pushed us

Into struggles
That led to understanding

He brought us to wild days
When we danced in celebration
And to tender nights
Spent in the embrace
Of a lover or a friend

He sent the times
When sorrow so pierced us
That we felt alone
Even in lively company

He offered Love
And the grief
Of losing loved ones

He asked us to explore
All the joys of the body's strength
And all the misery of the body's frailty

He urged us to action
That we could learn from success
And from failure

He revealed our fears
And our desires
Gave us the chance
To fully know ourselves
While we lived on earth

Then after we had filled ourselves
With life's intensity

Our horned Jehovah
Called us home

Imagine our surprise

As a child it was your habit
To lean toward my arm
Inhale deeply and say,
"Smells like sugar"

The sweetness yours
As it flowed like the river
Kissing all in its world to life

But like our western rivers
That do not reach the sea
You could not soothe yourself

Still, your sorrow and sweetness
Flow side by side
Remain separate

I pray that your kindness
Curl back to nourish you
As it calms and heals others

For I see your light reflect outward
Like the kerosene lantern
We lit when the power failed

The base of that lantern
Lay in its own shadow
It did not know its light

I hear the child I loved
In the voice of
The man on the phone
A man I can neither comfort
Nor advise

I love you
But I cannot follow you

I watch your journey
Unable to restrain or reform

We are one flesh
Our kinship lures me
Toward your darkness

I cannot follow
I must hold my own purposes
Hold myself

You will return
Only when you want to
Only when you can

The lesson is clear
One must not give up oneself
For another
Or both are doomed

The sky is gray while light dances
On the rapids in the river

It is not my place to want for you
What you do not want for yourself

I will wait on the shore

I miss you tonight
Have missed you
For more than a quarter century
Missed you
In the midst of family and friends

Love was your calling
Pain your companion
You were perfect for your purpose

So lovable that strangers were smitten
In the supermarket aisle
Their sudden grins
Flared up to meet your smile

You were small for your age
Sickness and surgeries had taken their toll
I knew the love
But I could not face the pain
Until you left

I wanted so much for you to live
I could not admit the price you paid
Only when you were dying did you whimper
Ask for the thing I could not give
Permission to flee the pain
Permission to depart this world

You left without permission
Taking everything
Giving everything
In one moment

The smallest cry
A moan repeated

The sound of the pain
Of a five-year-old

Struggling in a world
Beyond my reach

We share patterns
Habits of lineage
Chemistries of blood

Tales of my old sorrows
Cannot heal yours
Or free you
From the tangled threads
Of loss and longing
Yet I can offer you this
After years of sorrow
I am happy

This is the promise
Of the history and chemistry that tie us

The journey is toward joy

The quiet flow of time led me here
The continuing drip of days
Each with its gift
The song of the river
The patience of the cottonwoods
The help of friends

We walk the long path home
Until we find ourselves
As we are
Held in our own embrace

Small miracles weave the fabric of our lives
The used door you bought without thinking
Fits the doorway you didn't measure
The first peony of spring opens into a fuchsia softball
You return to find your wallet where you left it on the checkout counter
You think of a friend just before the phone rings

But along with these small miracles are the big ones
This is a story of three great miracles

I thought that the coyotes had eaten the turkey
I hadn't seen her in a month
I'd ceased even to think of her
Then she walked past my open door at dawn
Followed by ten cheeping balls of fluff
A miracle

She introduced them to the world
Showed them how to hide in the tall grass
Warmed them under her spreading body
They followed behind her long legs
She sang the soft trill of motherhood
As she brought them to greet me each morning

Four dawns later the cheeping was anguished
I heard the call that meant "Where are you?"
A universal call even humans recognize
The coyote had snatched their mother during the night
While she roosted on the ground
Her babies tucked under her wings
Throughout the day they called and searched
Returning again and again to the only other turkey in sight

The tom, a bird who spent his days in front of my windows
Watching his reflection as he strutted and gobbled
Turning his face blue above his red wattle cascade
He ignored other turkeys
Wanted only the admiration of humans
The babies followed this tom
Followed and pleaded

At dusk it rained
The rain brought a cold night
Cold enough to kill the motherless poults
I searched helplessly in the darkness
Until I had to give up
At first light I found the tight-packed ball
That broke into ten cheeping chicks
A second miracle

The third miracle was the greatest of all
On the second day of pleading
The tom moved away from my windows
He began walking with the babies
He called them to him
He gathered them
Lowered himself gently to warm and protect them
He made a hen's calls of warning, direction,
And contentment
Again I heard the soft trill of motherhood
His shape grew rounder, lower
No trace of wattles or blued face
He found purpose
Greater than his own beauty

I write the journey toward letting go
I write to shape the clouds within my mind
I write to begin the long knitting of the unknown

Before Rama and Hanuman fought Ravana
Before Krishna left the gopis to become king
Before the Buddha sat under the Bodhi tree
Murugan followed his consorts
To their home in Lanka
He brought his energy to that land
His power lingers in a jungle
Near the southern coast
Its focus is a small temple, Kataragama
A place of pilgrimage
Where humans go to ask for miracles

They must offer something in return
Murugan is a horse trader
A warrior, a fighter
The god of desire, ambition, action
His names are many
Skanda, Kumara, Kartikeya, Murugan, Subrahmanya
The one most familiar to me is Mars

In that temple
The man I had married
Asked for land and a child
In return he promised to build a temple
He received his boon and more
Through odd turns of fate
We found ourselves with
Fifty acres and four children
But no temple followed
In the time of triumph
The promise was not kept

Either we believe in the old gods
Or we do not
If we only believe until we get our desires,
We are arrogant and foolish
We cannot cheat the gods
This world is not a metaphor
Energies, no matter how we envision them,
Hold power

Four years after making the promise
We went to Tamil Nadu
A land that honors Murugan
Where men live amid his energies
Pray in ancient temples
My husband began drinking steadily
A habit that would define his next quarter century

We received the boon
But we were cursed
Our marriage soured
We entered hell worlds
Became lost to each other
And to ourselves
The land lay fallow
The magical children
Lived in a home filled with darkness
Anger twisting us all

I gathered posters and statues
Not a temple
Small symbols of respect

Enough to secure
Divorce from the darkness
I left the land

Years followed each other
Nothing in the lives of gods
But decades in the lives of men
My youngest child
Came with her daughter
Knew the story
Saw the posters
Understood, acted

In a cave on a hillside
Overlooking the land
She gathered
The posters and statues
She placed pieces of our history
She took fruit and flowers and incense
And made a temple

She prayed
She honored the promise
Then returned
To her life, her place

Now I am the keeper of the temple
Tonight at sunset I climb to the cave
Carrying a large red stone
And an apple
For red is Murugan's color

I lay them with the other offerings
I look out over the land
A beaver floats in the river
The low sun lights
The red cliffs of Copper Canyon

I feel the energy here
Talk to this energy
Let it hold me
I call that energy Murugan
I call it Mars
I am grateful

MY DREAM, MY LAND, MY HOME

I spent three years
Looking for the land
Days when I thought
I should settle for less
Days when I doubted

Then I found it waiting
More beautiful than my dream
The price, twice what I wanted to pay
I tried to turn away
But I was under its spell
I could not turn from myself

The land insisted I build
A beautiful house
Instead of the hut
I had planned
It demanded a home
That honored its full spirit
And my own

I slowly came
To belong to this land
To its depth and delight

I return to this lesson
When I believe I am not worthy
Of my dreams

I am the same being
I have always been
Though the story
Has changed
Over time

When I release the story
I become free

The rumpled man chose Chris
From the multitude
On the downtown sidewalk

He thrust a small pill bottle
Toward my friend
With a plea
"I don't have enough money
For my medicine"

Chris pulled three neatly folded bills
From his pocket
As the afternoon crowd broke around us
He offered them

The exchange complete
We rejoined the flow
"Xanax," Chris laughed softly

We have all known someone
Who needed to take the edge off

We have all stood on the corner
Where desire and danger meet

You don't ask to be born, and then they make you pay rent to stay.
—my friend Mark

The delicate drop of your wrist
Your graceful step
Your lithe body radiating blond light
I loved you with a hopeless love
That you accepted but could not return

You had many talents
The greatest your compassion
You loved expansively
"Many of them just want to be held,"
You said of your clients

The ads in the *Berkeley Barb* brought phone calls
From men who needed love
1969, a year of motorcycles and theater in the streets
San Francisco held a hidden danger
For a man who sold love

You did not know that paying the rent
Would cost you your life

Remember those
Who died as children
Your brother, your daughter
What do you remember about them?
Do you remember their light?

Those who left as teenagers
Your cousin, your grandson,
Your friend
Were they special from the start?

Those in their twenties
The man in your class
Your mentor
Were you struck by their kindness?
Their lack of ego?

Even in their thirties
Do you remember
Their gentleness, their honesty?

What was different
About those who left this world early?

Leaving us here with each other
But without their love

You are
The Great Destroyer

How do we
Understand
The attraction
We feel?
What is this longing
To dance with you?

We are not in the midst of a drug crisis
We are in the midst of a pain crisis
"Mild euphoria," they say
Have these experts never used drugs?
Opiates do not offer happiness
They stop pain

Painkillers

Stopping pain
Is not pleasure

We carry so much pain
That we are willing to sacrifice
Job, home, family, life itself
To dull that pain

We are people awash in pain

The grief
The grief is infinite
We laugh
Though we want to cry

We laugh
And shake our heads
To staunch the unshed tears
The inner sobbing

The grief is infinite
We clutch our hearts
In cupped hands
As if to watch
Our blood drip before us

The grief is infinite
We laugh
Shake our heads
Thrust our hearts back into
Our aching chests
Prepare to live our lives
Because we must

We see photos of thousands
Celebrating in the streets
We feel the same

Like dancing
Like crying
Freed from a burden
We did not know we carried
Until it was lifted

Our government's cruelty
Directed at the powerless
Touched all of us
Even the "lucky" ones

Our nation
Built on stolen land
By the labor of slaves
Voted on hate

At last, at last
After hundreds of years
By the thinnest of margins
Hate lost

They are surprised
That a nation stolen through genocide
Whose founding fathers
Owned slaves
Shows violence
On cell phone videos

They are shocked
That not only are young Black men
Killed without reason
But the rich and powerful
Must hide under their desks
Until they are led to safety

They are amazed to find
The fruits of history
Ripening at last

I am astonished that we did not see this coming

The tom turkeys strut and puff
Wing feathers scrape the ground
Tail feathers sweep from side to side
Like the queen's hand

The hens neither puff nor strut
They lack a cascade of red wattles
They cannot turn their faces blue
They ignore the toms' endless posturing
Peck at the preening suitors

The largest, most beautiful tom
The turkey who has bent
The other tom's necks beneath his own
The acknowledged leader
Goes out to meet the coyote when she comes
Goes to cow her with his beauty

She carries him off
Leaving only those beautiful feathers
Scattered on the ground

It brings the sins we thought we had shed
Wrapped in sorrow

The scapegoat always comes home

My ancestors were immigrants
Generation after generation
They left their homes
Searching for the Promised Land
Restless pursuit
Of adventure, peace, abundance

Lured by their dreams
They roamed
Each generation moving on

They crossed the Atlantic
They continued west
Across the continent
Arrived at last at the Pacific coast

My parents left that shore
For the Philippines
Where they became casualties in the Great War
Placed in a concentration camp
The urge for *farther* was starved out of them
They returned home
Looking for *safety*

I was born to both wanderlust and fear
The lessons of lineage are stronger
Than the choices of a single life
While hunger for something different drove me
Fear was my companion on the journey

Years of seeking
Led to understanding

There is nowhere else to go
Wherever we are
Is the Promised Land

I never thought
I would see
People who looked like me
Huddled in subways
In fear for their lives
Their elegant apartments
Destroyed by bombs
Owners of nice cars
At the border
Fleeing the carnage
Poignant op-eds
In graceful English
Detailing fear and grief

My world is upended

I have spent a lifetime
Witnessing families of color
Devastated by violence

I have seen people
Without cars
Without shoes
People who cannot write
Unable to flee
Or having fled turned back
At the border
Torn from the children
They hoped to save

Their suffering seems normal
It happens daily, for years on end
It happens nearby and far away

But always feels distant
Ukraine feels immediate
I recognize the children's snowsuits

My fortress walls
Have been pierced
I feel afraid

Security
Has been
A given
Wealth
Education
White skin

It's suddenly clear
I was never secure

Accepting suffering
In those who seem different
Allows suffering
To become normal
Allows it to grow
Until it arrives at
Our doorstep

I still do not expect war
In my streets
But I am less certain

Of everything

She said that hikers who could not read the land itself
Were already in too much danger
She said that those who needed cairns
Should not go into the wilderness

I remember the woman who broke her leg
Above the first cairn
Her partner hiked out to call 911
He said they were by the school
We drove up and down in emergency vehicles, looking
Exhausted, about to give up,
We tried the trail farthest from the school
We found him there frantic

I understood why she knocked down the cairns

The sky is gray
The grass is brown
The tree trunks black
A fire burns in the stove
To repel the cold
The day feels like death

I have watched the turning seasons
Through passing years
Thus I have no doubt
That winter passes

In the coldest, darkest days
Of the year
We greet our friends with
"Merry Christmas!"
"Happy New Year!"

This is how we practice
For dying

Your death was
Forty-four years ago
Today

I read your poem
"A Dog Has Died"
Felt the parade of death
That precedes us
The longing that binds us
To that parade

Can you feel our love?
Do you leap with joy
In a heaven
You did not expect?

Do you have a beautiful tail
Flowing out behind you?

Taking my place
In the rush-hour line
While coral and violet clouds
Rest above blue hills

Outlaw Country radio, 107.5
Intones a chorus
Of human joy and suffering

Called by sweetness and sorrow
My cells begin to fill with light
The love each nucleus has for its electrons
The love my hands have for the steering wheel
The love my eyes have for the crimson sky
The love that sky has for its fading clouds
The love of my tires for the pavement

My hands dissolve
And the steering wheel dissolves
And the sky dissolves
And the clouds dissolve
And the long line of cars
And all the tires
And the tears on my face
And the fading light in the sky
We all become love

All becoming each other
All becoming one
On the long drive home

The cat wakes me
Pleading to come inside
Water pours from the roof
It is raining in January

One hundred thirty dry days
Broken by rain
In the coldest season
Of the year

As miraculous as
A plague of locusts
The parting of the Red Sea

Rain in January
Surely the hand of God
Is moving over the land

The heron
Stands in
The river
Stillness
Within the
Glint and glisten
Of water racing
To the sea
She is pure
Focus
Surrounded by
The clamor
Of the river song
She draws
Its tumult
Into her perfect silence

The snag is full of vultures
Drying their wings
Pulling at their feathers
After the rain

What death or dying
Has brought so many
To a tree
They never visit?

Limited to the moment
Between birth and death

In the embrace of Spirit
Debility transforms into
The voice of the Infinite

Frailty becomes the launchpad
To the limitless
From the prison of the known

It isn't strength
My Social Security checks
Are reminders that age
Has stolen strength

It isn't precision
A tremor sloshes the tea
In my cup

It is magic

When the ax
Swings down
In its great arc
The log reveals
Its naked heart

The log, the ax, and I
Are one
Within the circle of a spell

A glimpse of the morning star
Is a special gift
Venus leading
Rather than trailing
The sun

Unlike the evening star
It has no wish-granting power
It offers no reward
Other than itself

Quiet
Private
Bidding me good journey
As I travel into the day

After a decade
My feet still know the path
Soon my eyes find landmarks

At the top a ring of stone slabs
Rise to form a sanctuary
Gaps open toward
The long flank of Black Mesa
And the red cliffs of Copper Canyon
The stones form natural nichos
Hold offerings
Left by strangers

The thumb of rock rises from a mesa
Unusual in both shape and energy
This is where I found the pot sherd
When I was worrying about my jailed son
This is where I saw a peacock
Its long tail dragging
This is where I glued a sequined image
Of the Virgen de Guadalupe
To the cliff edge
Its bright-green sequins
Visible from far off

Today I look for La Madre
Nothing remains but some dozen sequins
Bleached by years in the sun
A box in the largest nicho
Has crumbled
Leaving its gift of shells on the dirt

Unknown pilgrims
Self-taught pagans
I too offer my respect
To the energy of this place

I do not know or question
Why I bring my gifts
A wand of lavender stalks
A book of poetry
I place my offerings with the shells

Looping memories arc back and back
Connections form
Weave personal patterns
A skein of love

Holding my mother's hand
Keeps my hand higher than my head
While we walk to the mailbox
Waiting at the end of the gravel road
Which will be paved before
I am old enough to ride a bicycle

My father runs behind my blue bike
Supporting me
Until he feels my balance
He quietly removes his hand
Still running so that I do not notice
My freedom

Do you think anyone will want this bike?
The tires have gone flat
I have not ridden it for years
Though I loved it when I bought it
After seeing the listing
On the message board
In front of Trader Joe's

Long ago
Before the days of Craigslist

I am still the child
Who sits in awe
Watching the industry of ants

The years fall
Like autumn leaves
Billowing torrents
Cushioning mounds

I can jump from the roof
And land safely

I sit in bed watching videos
Of Tibetans telling stories
About the Tertön Chögyam Trungpa
Who unearthed treasures
Left by Padmasambhava

They show the cave where
Parchment scripture fell from the ceiling
And where they helped to dig up
The stone box that held a statue of the Buddha

Each treasure offered spiritual direction
Guidance that had waited
Until it was needed
Energy hidden for two thousand years

Miracles in Tibet
Watched from my bed
In New Mexico
Miracle upon miracle

Space and time
Now erased
By an energy
We have named
Electronics

Two elders
Side by side
Lost in their smartphones

"How sweet to sit by you, my love!"

Or perhaps tomorrow
Or any other day
But you will certainly die

In the midst of a happy life
Or while longing
For the unattainable
Or while suffering

The moment will come
A moment of shock
When you know
In every cell
"This is what I feared"

You will be filled
With the understanding
Of what you could not have believed
One moment earlier

You will find yourself standing
On both sides
Of the unimaginable chasm
The infinite gulf that separates
Imprisonment in flesh
From the freedom of eternity

You will be astounded
When you choose freedom

Ducks startle
With raucous quacking
And a noisy flapping
Of wings

But the black flight
Of ravens
As they rise together
From the river's edge
Is soundless

Not one caw
Breaks the air

In the face of danger
They agree

Silence

We pass yards filled with old cars
Waiting to offer parts
Yards filled with logs
Building materials or firewood?
Stacks of pallets
Perfect for some project
Sometime

The same treasures wait
Back home, under a desert sun
While here a cold drizzle
Glistens on wood and metal

The rusting cars and the pallets are a comfort
After my days
In the neat order
Of California
How do Californians find parts for their cars?
Or build chicken coops?

In Winter cold and darkness
I dream of the light and opening of Spring
I gaze at the calendar
Counting the days till Easter,
Which is my beacon

Pounded by Spring winds
I dream of the flat heat of Summer
Counting the days till the Fourth of July,
Which is my beacon

In the heat and frenzy of Summer
I long for the cheer of Fall
I gaze at the calendar
Counting the days till Thanksgiving,
Which is my beacon

In the boisterous triumph of Fall
I long for the calm quiet of winter
I gaze at the calendar
Counting the days till Christmas,
Which is my beacon

Thus the wheel of the year turns
Propelled by longing

Rain
Snow
Hail

The clouds are dark
The wind is brutal

I would never
Have imagined
That I could get
So much pleasure
From such grievous weather

I remember the summer
When I danced with friends
On the patio
When the flowers leaped from the ground
In all their glowing excitement
When I brought baskets of tomatoes
To the young man
Who loved me

Why did I walk away
From that love?
From those vegetables, flowers and friends—
To embrace loneliness, struggle, mistakes?

I left because I wanted more

Who can explain the motion that compels us?
What in us demands that we grow?

Historians may write of this year
They will not write of the hum of bees
In the branches of lavender
Or of the cottonwood leaves
Shimmering in the morning light
The will not care about
The sweet beauty of
Baby chicks

Historians may write of wealthy pedophiles
Who grow old and rich
In the company of men of power
They may write about children torn from parents
Waiting in squalid prisons
They may write about parents
Afraid for sons and daughters
Who could be killed
At any moment for any reason

When the historians write their treatises
Will they hear the buzz of pollinators in the plants?
Or will they hear only the sound of fighting
As hatred begets hatred
And greed turns back upon itself?

Will the delight and the horror
Continue to balance precariously?
Or will the flood of karma
Sweep away more than
The bees and lavender
The sunlight and the trees?

I have seen them
Walking on the side of the road
Some with backpacks
Others with bags clutched
To their chests
Or hanging from their shoulders

Today I am walking on the side of road
Cars race by
They do not stop
I am buffeted by their winds

I want to explain that
I am looking for my cell phone
I want a sign that says "Do not pity me"
A sign that says "I am like you"

I wonder if the homeless
Who walk
In this land of cars
Want signs like the ones I desire
While their signs read
"Hungry"
"Need work"

When did that phrase shift
From a reason for respect
To a call for pity?

What the river said
I am Flow
Always and only water
Life itself
Not merely the chemistry that supports life
But the movement that is life
I am in cells and I am the nourishment for cells
I call to myself in the blood of beavers
Swimming upstream
The trunk of the cottonwoods on the banks
I whisper to myself in all life as I flow by
You will join me when Time calls to you
For time is the river in which I flow
We will trade places times beyond number
Inside, outside, always moving

What the lake said
I am Peace
Always and only water
Held in the hills' embrace
Resting while moving
The life that rests in me ripples in the currents
Stillness in endless flow

What the rain said
I am Joy
Always and only water
Gathering into myself
Through communion
My first essence too small to be seen

Uniting with my fellows until heavy enough to fall
Bringing the joy of the heavens to earth

I am water

We call on the lords of light
And on the lords of darkness:
Bend toward us
Listen to our prayer
Now and at the moment of our death

Are we not always dying?
The past ripped from our clutches
By the journey into what will be
While we try to hold on to
Our attachments
And our passions

Called upon to let the old die
For the sake of the new
The selves we know and have known
Dying for the sake of an unknowable future

Cradle us, hold us close
For we are always dying

When the wind whispers
The secrets of its travels
We cannot bear to sit quietly
And listen

We worship the sun

Not some idea about the sun
Not a theory
Not a story
The sun itself
Warming our faces
Cleansing our hearts
Strengthening our bodies
As we turn toward its light

On the day of greatest darkness
When our longing is boundless
We celebrate
Our certainty
That the deepest darkness
Begins the long journey
Toward light

We give thanks
We offer praise
We worship the sun

The silence is deep
The moon dark
Stoke the fire
Make resolutions
Sleep

What is this feeling?
Less solid than sadness
Perhaps wistful
"A vague regret or longing"

If I understood what I longed for
I could lament
Or act

But the clouds of feeling
Dissolve when I reach
To grasp them

My hands on the keyboard
Are stiff
Look worn

The world is beguiling
But it is not enough

I am walking by the river
Under a sky so blue that my heart cracks open
The last green of summer is flecked
With the first yellow of fall

The river glistens after last night's rain
Two ducks trace circles on the water
Paddling just enough to stay out of reach

My senses catch fire
My mind turns to Mary Oliver
She would know how to write of the wonder
How to balance the longing with contentment
To call forth both the exuberant beauty
And the web of love from which it arises

She could craft words as beautiful as this moment
But I am the one walking by the river

Dust drifts slowly
In the quiet

Footsteps make no sound
No shape is recognized

Everything is
Nothing is described

The silence of writer's block
Beauty with her face turned inward

A teeny slice of time
Expanding out and out
Until all beings
In all dimensions
In all histories
And futures
Rest

ACKNOWLEDGMENTS

Ginger Legato designed the manuscript for publication. She held it with patience and skill. Moreover she held me with kindness.

Marie Landau edited the manuscript. Her skill transformed my efforts.

Lesley Poling-Kempes gathers the Abiquiu writers around her. She creates community and calls it a class.

The Abiquu Inn provides the writers and artisits of Abiquiu a place to share and sell their work.

Diana Lanier has given me encouragement and direction. She has both pushed and pulled me on my way.

My children and grandchildren have shown me love: Jim, Will, Anita, Emily, Colten, Zoe, Ila, Ardrie, Florence, and Kaleb.

Thank you.

ABOUT THE AUTHOR

Oro Lynn Benson has lived in northern New Mexico, making her home along the mighty Chama River for over 45 years. She writes from the deep empathy that her years as a mother, a nurse, vedic astrologer and poet have brought her.

Her first book of poems *Love, Death, and Flowing Water,* reflects the days and seasons of river life— the wild, the serene, and the qualities of beauty she extracts from her singular sense of place and communion with the land. In her newest book, *Because of the Sands of Time,* Oro Lynn continues her exploration of time and spirit, grief, gladness, and the surprises revealed in silence.

WHY

I write the journey toward letting go
I write to shape the clouds within my mind
I write to begin the long knitting of the unknown

ABIQUIU PRESS

abquiupress@gmail.com